NUMBER
Your
DAYS
and
GROW WISE
A Daily Planner

ACTIVINOTES

Activinotes
DAILY JOURNALS, PLANNERS, NOTEBOOKS AND OTHER BLANK BOOKS

All Rights reserved. No part of this book may be reproduced or used in any way or form or by any means whether electronic or mechanical, this means that you cannot record or photocopy any material ideas or tips that are provided in this book.

Copyright 2016

Date: ____________

Time: **Appointment:**

DATE: ____________

TIME: | **APPOINTMENT:**

DATE: ______________

TIME: **APPOINTMENT:**

DATE: ____________

TIME:	APPOINTMENT:

DATE: ______________

TIME: **APPOINTMENT:**

DATE: ____________

TIME:	**APPOINTMENT:**

DATE: ____________

TIME: **APPOINTMENT:**

DATE: ____________

TIME:	APPOINTMENT:

DATE: ______________

TIME: **APPOINTMENT:**

DATE: ____________

TIME: | **APPOINTMENT:**

DATE: ______________

TIME: **APPOINTMENT:**

DATE: ____________

TIME: **APPOINTMENT:**

DATE: ______________

TIME: **APPOINTMENT:**

DATE: ____________

TIME: | **APPOINTMENT:**

DATE: ____________

TIME: APPOINTMENT:

DATE: ____________

TIME: | **APPOINTMENT:**

DATE: ______________

TIME: **APPOINTMENT:**

DATE: ____________

TIME: **APPOINTMENT:**

DATE: ______________

TIME: **APPOINTMENT:**

DATE: ______________

TIME: | **APPOINTMENT:**

DATE: ______________

TIME: APPOINTMENT:

DATE: ______________

TIME: | **APPOINTMENT:**

DATE: ______________

TIME: **APPOINTMENT:**

DATE: ____________

TIME: **APPOINTMENT:**

DATE: ______________

TIME: **APPOINTMENT:**

DATE: ____________

TIME: **APPOINTMENT:**

Date: ____________

Time: **Appointment:**

DATE: ____________

TIME: APPOINTMENT:

DATE: ______________

TIME: APPOINTMENT:

DATE: ____________

TIME: **APPOINTMENT:**

DATE: ______________

TIME: **APPOINTMENT:**

DATE: ____________

TIME: **APPOINTMENT:**

DATE: ____________

TIME: **APPOINTMENT:**

DATE: ______________

TIME: **APPOINTMENT:**

DATE: ______________

TIME:	**APPOINTMENT:**

DATE: ____________

TIME: **APPOINTMENT:**

DATE: ______________

TIME: APPOINTMENT:

DATE: ____________

TIME: **APPOINTMENT:**

DATE: ______________

TIME: **APPOINTMENT:**

DATE: ____________

TIME: | **APPOINTMENT:**

DATE: ______________

TIME: APPOINTMENT:

DATE: ____________

TIME:	**APPOINTMENT:**

DATE: ____________

TIME: **APPOINTMENT:**

DATE: ______________

TIME: **APPOINTMENT:**

DATE: ______________

TIME: **APPOINTMENT:**

DATE: ____________

TIME:	**APPOINTMENT:**

DATE: ____________

TIME: **APPOINTMENT:**

DATE: ____________

TIME: | APPOINTMENT:

DATE: ____________

TIME: **APPOINTMENT:**

DATE: ____________

TIME: | **APPOINTMENT:**

DATE: ______________

TIME: APPOINTMENT:

DATE: ______________

TIME: APPOINTMENT:

DATE: ______________

TIME: **APPOINTMENT:**

DATE: ______________

TIME: **APPOINTMENT:**

DATE: ____________

TIME: **APPOINTMENT:**

DATE: ____________

TIME: **APPOINTMENT:**

DATE: ______________

TIME: **APPOINTMENT:**

DATE: ____________

TIME: **APPOINTMENT:**

DATE: ____________

TIME: **APPOINTMENT:**

DATE: ______________

TIME: **APPOINTMENT:**

DATE: ______________

TIME: **APPOINTMENT:**

DATE: ____________

TIME:	**APPOINTMENT:**

DATE: ____________

TIME: APPOINTMENT:

DATE: ___________

TIME: APPOINTMENT:

DATE: ____________

TIME: **APPOINTMENT:**

DATE: ____________

TIME: | **APPOINTMENT:**

DATE: ______________

TIME: **APPOINTMENT:**

DATE: ____________

TIME: APPOINTMENT:

DATE: ____________

TIME: **APPOINTMENT:**

DATE: ____________

TIME: APPOINTMENT:

DATE: ____________

TIME: APPOINTMENT:

DATE: ____________

TIME: **APPOINTMENT:**

DATE: ____________

TIME: **APPOINTMENT:**

DATE: ______________

TIME: **APPOINTMENT:**

DATE: ____________

TIME: APPOINTMENT:

DATE: ______________

TIME: APPOINTMENT:

DATE: ______________

TIME: **APPOINTMENT:**

DATE: ____________

TIME: **APPOINTMENT:**

DATE: ______________

TIME: **APPOINTMENT:**

DATE: ____________

TIME: APPOINTMENT:

DATE: ______________

TIME: **APPOINTMENT:**

DATE: ____________

TIME: APPOINTMENT:

DATE: ______________

TIME: **APPOINTMENT:**

DATE: ___________

TIME: **APPOINTMENT:**

DATE: ____________

TIME: **APPOINTMENT:**

DATE: ____________

TIME: **APPOINTMENT:**

DATE: ____________

TIME: APPOINTMENT:

DATE: ______________

TIME: | **APPOINTMENT:**

DATE: ____________

TIME:	APPOINTMENT:

DATE: ______________

TIME: **APPOINTMENT:**

DATE: ______________

TIME: **APPOINTMENT:**

DATE: ____________

TIME: **APPOINTMENT:**

DATE: ______________

TIME:	**APPOINTMENT:**

DATE: ____________

TIME: **APPOINTMENT:**

DATE: ____________

TIME: **APPOINTMENT:**

DATE: ____________

TIME: **APPOINTMENT:**

DATE: ______________

TIME: **APPOINTMENT:**

DATE: ____________

TIME:	**APPOINTMENT:**

DATE: ______________

TIME: **APPOINTMENT:**

DATE: ____________

TIME: | **APPOINTMENT:**

DATE: ____________

TIME: **APPOINTMENT:**

DATE: ____________

TIME: **APPOINTMENT:**

DATE: ______________

TIME: APPOINTMENT:

DATE: ____________

TIME:	**APPOINTMENT:**

www.ingramcontent.com/pod-product-compliance
Lightning Source LLC
Chambersburg PA
CBHW080737250626
47170CB00010B/2862
* 9 7 8 1 6 8 3 2 1 2 3 2 4 *